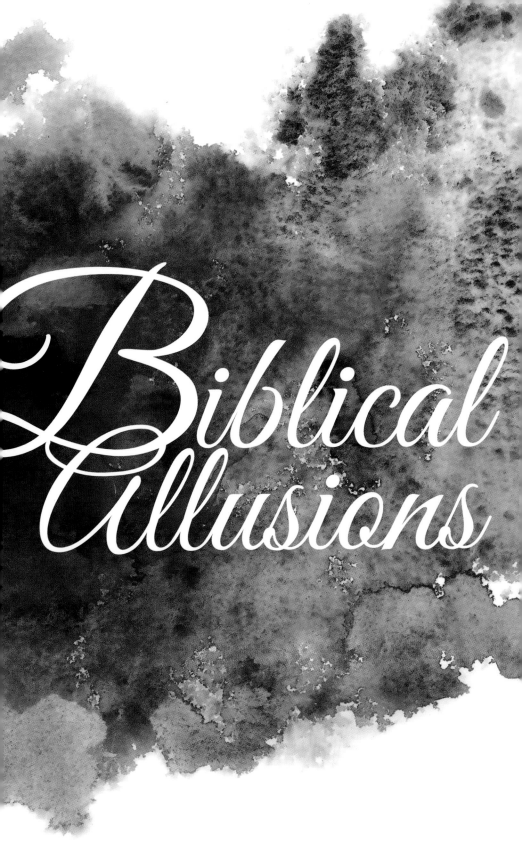

Biblical Allusions

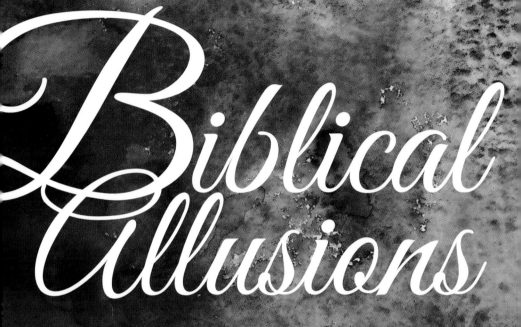

Biblical Allusions

Essential Literary Themes

by Lindsay Bacher

Essential Library

An Imprint of Abdo Publishing | abdopublishing.com

abdopublishing.com

Published by Abdo Publishing, a division of ABDO, PO Box 398166, Minneapolis, Minnesota 55439. Copyright © 2016 by Abdo Consulting Group, Inc. International copyrights reserved in all countries. No part of this book may be reproduced in any form without written permission from the publisher. Essential Library™ is a trademark and logo of Abdo Publishing.

Printed in the United States of America, North Mankato, Minnesota
052015
092015

Cover Photo: Shutterstock Images
Interior Photos: Shutterstock Images, 1; Geraint Lewis/Rex Features/AP Images, 13; Walt Disney Pictures/Photofest, 15, 19, 21, 28; Walt Disney Pictures/Everett Collection, 17, 79; Bettmann/Corbis, 23; Warner Bros./Photofest, 33, 35, 43, 47, 49; Warner Bros./Everett Collection, 37, 39, 41, 50; Columbia/Everett Collection, 55, 57; Everett Collection, 59, 63; Columbia Pictures/Photofest, 65; iStockphoto, 67, 95; Mary Evans/Two Arts Ltd. Ronald Grant/Everett Collection, 71, 72; Buena Vista Pictures/Everett Collection, 81, 84, 87, 92; Mary Evans/Pixar/Disney/Ronald Grant/Everett Collection, 89

Editor: Mari Kesselring
Series Designer: Maggie Villaume

Library of Congress Control Number: 2015931042
Cataloging-in-Publication Data

Bacher, Lindsay.
 Biblical allusions / Lindsay Bacher.
  p. cm. -- (Essential literary themes)
Includes bibliographical references and index.
ISBN 978-1-62403-802-0
1. American literature--Themes, motives--Juvenile literature. 2. American literature--History and criticism--Juvenile literature.   I. Title.
810--dc23

                                                                    2015931042

Contents

1

INTRODUCTION TO
Themes in Literature

$\mathcal{D}$o you find yourself drawn to the same types of stories? Are your favorite characters on a quest? Are they seeking revenge? Or are your favorite stories about love? Love, revenge, a quest—these are all examples of themes. Although each story is different, many stories focus on similar themes. You can expand your understanding of the books you read by recognizing the common themes within them.

What Is a Theme?

A theme is a concept or idea that shows up again and again in various works of art, literature, music, theater, film, and other endeavors throughout history. Some themes revolve around a story's plot. For example, a play about a young girl moving away from home and learning the ways of the world would be considered a coming of age story. But themes are not always so easily noticed. For example, a work might have allusions. Allusions are references, sometimes indirect, to other works or historical events. Themes might also relate to specific characters or subjects of a work. For example, many stories present heroes or villains. These common character types are often called archetypes.

How Do You Uncover a Theme?

Themes are presented in different ways in different works, so you may not always be aware of them. Many works have multiple themes. Uncover themes by asking yourself questions about the work. What is the main point or lesson of the story? What is the main conflict? What do the characters want? Where does the story take place? In many cases, themes may not be apparent until after a close study, or analysis, of the text.

What Is an Analysis?

Writing an analysis allows you to explore the themes in a work. In an analysis, you can consider themes in multiple ways. You can describe what themes are present in a work. You can compare one work to another to see how the presentation of a theme differs between the two forms. You can see how the use of a particular theme either supports or rejects society's norms. Rather than attempt to discover the author's purpose in creating a work, an analysis reveals what *you* see in the work.

Raising your awareness of themes through analysis allows you to dive deeper into the work itself. You may begin to see similarities between all creative works that you encounter. You may also improve your own writing by expanding your understanding of how stories use themes to engage readers.

Forming a Thesis

Form your questions about how a theme is presented in a work or multiple works and find answers within the work itself. Then you can create a thesis. The thesis is the key point in your analysis. It is your argument about the work. For example, if you want to argue that the theme of a book is love, your thesis could be worded as follows: Allison Becket's novel *On the Heartless Road* asserts that receiving love is critical to the human experience.

How to Make a Thesis Statement

In an analysis, a thesis statement typically appears at the end of the introductory paragraph. It is usually only one sentence long and states the author's main idea.

Providing Evidence

Once you have formed a thesis, you must provide evidence to support it. Evidence will usually take the form of examples and quotations from the work itself, often including dialogue from a character. You may wish to address what others have written about the work. Quotes from these individuals may help support your claim. If you find any quotes or examples that contradict your thesis, you will need to create an argument against them. For instance: Many critics claim the theme of love is secondary to that of revenge, as the main character, Carly, sabotages the lives of her loved ones throughout the novel. However, the novel's resolution proves that Carly's experience with love is the key to her humanity.

Concluding the Essay

After you have written several arguments and included evidence to support them, finish the essay with

How to Support a Thesis Statement

An analysis should include several arguments that support the thesis's claim. An argument is one or two sentences long and is supported by evidence from the work being discussed. Organize the arguments into paragraphs. These paragraphs make up the body of the analysis.

a conclusion. The conclusion restates the ideas from the thesis and summarizes some of the main points from the essay. The conclusion's final thought often considers additional implications for the essay or gives the reader something to ponder further.

How to Conclude an Essay

Begin your conclusion with a recap of the thesis and a brief summary of the most important or strongest arguments. Leave readers with a final thought that puts the essay in a larger context or considers its wider implications.

In This Book

In this book, you will read summaries of works, each followed by an analysis. Critical thinking sections will give you a chance to consider other theses and questions about the work. Did you agree with the author's analysis? What other questions are raised by the thesis and its arguments? You can also see other directions the author could have pursued to analyze the work. Then, in the Analyze It section in the final pages of this book, you will have an opportunity to create your own analysis paper.

The Theme of Biblical Allusions

The book you are reading focuses on the theme of biblical allusions. Biblical allusions are a common literary technique an author uses to draw a parallel between the work and the Bible. The Bible is a holy book for Christians. Many works of literature, film, and art reference the Bible to add a layer of depth to the story. For example, the phrase *promised land* originates from the books of Genesis and Exodus in the Bible. In those stories, God promises Abraham a safe place for his family—the Promised Land. After freeing the Israelites (the descendants of Abraham), from the pharaoh and slavery in Egypt, Moses leads them through the desert toward the Promised Land. Many authors use the term *promised land* to refer to the idea of a safe haven reached at the end of a long journey.

Look for the Guides

Throughout the chapters that analyze the works, thesis statements have been highlighted. The box next to the thesis helps explain what questions are being raised about the work. Supporting arguments have also been highlighted. The boxes next to the arguments help explain how these points support the thesis. The conclusions are also accompanied by explanatory boxes. Look for these guides throughout each analysis.

2

AN OVERVIEW OF

The Lion, the Witch and the Wardrobe

The author of *The Lion, the Witch and the Wardrobe*, C. S. Lewis, was one of the most famous Christian authors of the 1900s. Lewis wrote many nonfiction books, including *Mere Christianity*, *The Screwtape Letters*, *A Grief Observed*, and a memoir, *Surprised by Joy*. He was a well-known Christian apologetic, rationally arguing the theology of Christianity against atheism or agnosticism. The seven books in the Chronicles of Narnia series are C. S. Lewis's only children's novels. He also wrote three adult novels, *Out of the Silent Planet*, *Perelandra*, and *That Hideous Strength*. These three novels make up the

The Lion, the Witch and the Wardrobe presents a fantasy world with many unique characters.

Space Trilogy, a science fiction trilogy that has many Christian themes.

The World of Narnia

The Lion, the Witch and the Wardrobe is set in World War II England. Siblings Peter, Susan, Edmond, and Lucy Pevensie leave London to live in the countryside with the Professor. As the children explore his house, Lucy steps inside a large wardrobe and is transported to the snowy land of Narnia. There, Lucy meets Mr. Tumnus, a fawn, by a light post. She goes to his house for tea. Mr. Tumnus becomes overcome with guilt and reveals that he invited Lucy to his house to kidnap her and turn her over to the White Witch. Now friends with Mr. Tumnus, Lucy returns through the forest to the wardrobe. However, none of her siblings believe she traveled to Narnia.

A few days later, Lucy returns to Narnia through the wardrobe, and Edmond follows her. Edmond meets the Queen of Narnia (the White Witch), riding a giant sleigh. She bribes Edmond with turkish delights, a candy, asking him to bring his brother and two sisters back to Narnia. As he returns to the wardrobe, he meets Lucy, who is coming back from tea with Mr. Tumnus.

Mr. and Mrs. Beaver are two of the many fantastic creatures living in Narnia.

They return to the Professor's house through the wardrobe. Edmond pretends he was never in Narnia and Lucy is making it up.

Through the Wardrobe

One day, while hiding from the adults, all four children climb into the wardrobe and find themselves in Narnia. Lucy takes them to Mr. Tumnus's house, but it's been ransacked. There's a note posted that Mr. Tumnus has been arrested for treason and harboring spies. Lucy realizes that the White Witch thinks she is a spy. The children meet Mr. Beaver, a friend of Mr. Tumnus, who brings them to his house. Mrs. Beaver is there, and together Mr. and Mrs. Beaver feed them and tell the children about Mr. Tumnus's arrest. Lucy believes it's her fault Mr. Tumnus was arrested, and she wants to save him. But he's been turned to stone in the courtyard of the White Witch's house, where she keeps a collection of stone animals.

Aslan and the Stone Table

Mrs. and Mr. Beaver tell the children about the White Witch and Aslan the lion. The White Witch has cursed Narnia, making it always winter but never Christmas. Prophecy says that when two sons of Adam and two daughters of Eve (what Narnians call humans) sit on the thrones of Narnia, the White Witch's reign and life will be over. Aslan, who has been away from Narnia for several generations, is rumored to be returning to defeat the White Witch. Aslan is king of the wood, king of the beasts, and son of the Emperor-beyond-the-Sea. As the Beavers are telling this story, the children realize Edmond has disappeared and betrayed them to the White Witch. The Beavers convince the devastated Peter, Susan, and Lucy the only way to save Edmond is to travel to the Stone Table to meet Aslan. The group leaves at once.

Edmond travels to the White Witch's house, where he tells the White Witch about Aslan's return.

At first, the White Witch treats Edmond kindly.

Immediately the White Witch prepares her sleigh, and they ride out to find Peter, Susan, Lucy, and the Beavers. The White Witch treats Edmond cruelly, speaking harshly to him, tying his hands, and whipping him. Edmond regrets leaving his brother and sisters, realizing he has helped out the wrong side.

As the group travels to the Stone Table, they are surprised by Father Christmas. Aslan's return is causing the White Witch's magic to weaken, breaking the "always winter, never Christmas" curse. Father Christmas gives Susan, Lucy, and Peter presents to help in their fight against the White Witch. Peter receives a sword and shield for the battle. Susan is given a bow and horn. Lucy receives a healing potion. The group continues on to the Stone Table through the Narnia countryside, which is showing signs of spring.

Meeting Aslan

When they arrive at the Stone Table, Lucy, Susan, and Peter meet Aslan, who is joined by many other creatures ready to fight the White Witch. A wolf from the White Witch attacks Susan, but Peter uses his new sword to protect her and kill the wolf. Aslan sends a team of animals that rescue Edmond from the White Witch's camp moments before she was going to kill him.

The next day, the White Witch comes to the Stone Table to claim Edmond's life as price for his betrayal of Aslan. The White Witch is owed blood, or Narnia will be destroyed. Aslan and the White Witch confer privately for a long time. When their meeting is over, Aslan announces the White Witch has given up her claim on Edmond's life.

Aslan's Sacrifice

That night, Susan and Lucy can't sleep. They follow a very tired and somber Aslan through the woods, up to

Aslan saves Edmond from the White Witch.

the Stone Table. Aslan tells them to stay in the bushes
no matter what they see. When they get to the Stone
Table, the White Witch and her army of ogres and
hags are waiting there. Aslan surrenders himself to the
creatures freely, and they tie him up, cut his mane, and
mock him. Lucy and Susan watch in horror as the White
Witch stabs and kills Aslan, who gives himself up to her
without a fight.

After the White Witch leaves, Susan and Lucy sob
over the body of Aslan for hours. At sunrise, the girls
walk away from the body and hear a loud noise—the
Stone Table cracking. They find Aslan has risen from the

dead. He tells them, "when a willing victim who had committed no treachery was killed in a traitor's stead, the Table would crack and Death itself would start working backward."[1]

Full of energy and with Lucy and Susan on his back, Aslan runs the long distance to the White Witch's house and her courtyard of stone animals. Aslan's touch and breath unfreezes the stone animals, bringing them back to life. Lucy is reunited with Mr. Tumnus, and together with the rest of the animals, they rush back to the Stone Table to join the battle against the White Witch. Peter and Edmond are fighting the White Witch and her army, and Aslan joins the battle to defeat her once and for all.

The four siblings take their places on the four thrones at Narnia's castle, as Queen Susan, King Peter, Queen Lucy, and King Edmond. They rule Narnia for many years as wise and gracious kings and queens.

One day, they are riding in the woods and find a light post. They travel through the dense woods and find themselves again in the wardrobe and back in the Professor's house. The Professor, who seems to know more about Narnia than he lets on, tells them the gateway through the wardrobe is shut, but once a king in Narnia, always a king in Narnia.

Peter, along with his brother and sisters, fights against the White Witch in an epic battle.

3

C. S. Lewis and Author Intent

*W*hen looking for biblical allusions in a work, it can be helpful to consider a work from the author's perspective. You might study the author's background to try to determine if he or she intended to draw biblical allusions in a work. Some authors may purposely allude to stories from the Bible. Others may be indirectly influenced by biblical narratives. They may include allusions without realizing it. Studying author intent when looking for biblical allusions in a work can influence how you understand the work.

In *The Lion, the Witch and the Wardrobe*, Aslan is first whispered about as "King of the wood and the son of the great Emperor-beyond-the-Sea . . . *the* lion, the great Lion."[1] Throughout the story, biblical allusions

C. S. Lewis intended to include biblical allusions when he wrote
The Lion, the Witch and the Wardrobe.

Thesis Statement

At the end of the first paragraph, the author states her thesis: "Through the death and resurrection of Aslan in *The Lion, the Witch and the Wardrobe*, C. S. Lewis makes complex theological themes accessible to young adult audiences, following his career as an apologetic and Christian novelist." This essay argues that Lewis uses Aslan as a Christ figure to convey theological concepts to young readers.

Argument One

The author now specifically talks about biblical allusions and Aslan's construction as a Christ figure: "Unlike many other literary characters that have sacrificial deaths and resurrections, such as Harry Potter, Aslan's death and resurrection closely parallel Christ's." The author divides this argument among three paragraphs.

construct Aslan as a Christ figure, saving Narnia from the curse and cruelties of the White Witch. The author, C. S. Lewis, was well-known as a Christian apologetic. In his works for adults, Lewis argued in favor of Christianity. Through the death and resurrection of Aslan in *The Lion, the Witch and the Wardrobe*, C. S. Lewis makes complex theological themes accessible to young adult audiences, following his career as an apologetic and Christian novelist.

Unlike many other literary characters that have sacrificial deaths and resurrections, such as Harry Potter, Aslan's death and resurrection closely parallel Christ's. Aslan goes freely and willingly to the White Witch, knowing he is heading to his death at the Stone Table. This is similar to the story of Jesus's death in the Bible. In the Bible, after telling his disciples that he will be killed, Jesus laments in the Garden of Gethsemane and prays, "My Father, if this cannot pass unless I drink it, your will be done."[2] Jesus is telling God that he will not interfere with what God wants. Like Aslan, Jesus already knows the fate awaiting him. Yet he complies with the will of God and does not put up a fight when the Roman guards come for him. Both Jesus and Aslan have the power to stop their deaths and yet do not exercise it.

Theologically, Jesus sacrifices himself to redeem the sins of humanity, which were brought into the world through original sin in the Garden of Eden. This theological concept is the theory of atonement. Atonement means that humanity finds redemption through Jesus's sacrifice. Likewise, Aslan's death atones for Edmond's betrayal, fulfilling his blood debt to the White Witch. In their resurrections, both Jesus and Aslan conquer death, sin, and betrayal.

Aslan as a Christ figure is stronger than other literary characters who sacrifice themselves for others. Harry Potter, for example, willingly allows himself to be killed by Lord Voldemort. Because his mother sacrificed her life for his when was an infant, Harry does not actually die. But the larger framework of atonement makes Aslan a stronger Christ figure than Harry Potter. This allows for the young adult audience of *The Lion, the Witch and the Wardrobe* to understand, through biblical allusions, the deeper theological theme of atonement.

Argument Two

In her second argument, the author brings in Lewis's intent as an author: "According to Lewis, *The Lion, the Witch and the Wardrobe* imagines what Christ's sacrifice would be like in a fantasy world, and Lewis's own beliefs clearly influenced its construction."

According to Lewis, *The Lion, the Witch and the Wardrobe* imagines what Christ's sacrifice would be like in a fantasy world, and Lewis's own beliefs clearly influenced its construction. After the book was released, many readers wondered if Lewis meant it to be allegory that teaches readers a moral or religious lesson. In a letter to James E. Higgins of the *Horn Book Magazine*, Lewis wrote, "The Narnian books are not so much allegory as supposal. 'Suppose there were a Narnian world and it, like ours, needed redemption. What kind of incarnation and Passion might Christ be supposed to undergo *there*?'"[3] Lewis claims he did not intend for *The*

Lion, the Witch and the Wardrobe to be a direct allegorical retelling of the story of Jesus Christ. Instead, by placing the adventures of Susan, Lucy, Edmond, and Peter in a fantasy world, Lewis is able to take the broad outline of Christian theology into an entirely new context. He did not mean for his book to be an allegory. But the strong parallels that exist, influenced by Lewis's own beliefs, undeniably lead people to read *The Lion, the Witch and the Wardrobe* as one.

Lewis's Space Trilogy has similar biblical allusions and theological themes to *The Lion, the Witch and the Wardrobe*. Lewis spent many years teaching and writing Christian apologetics books. Lewis fills his science fiction novels with theological themes such as the origin of sin and the struggle between good and evil. Lewis once wrote, "Any amount of theology can now be smuggled into people's minds under the cover of romance without them knowing it."[4]

Lewis's long career writing nonfiction Christian essays and books and his own Christian beliefs

Argument Three

Here the author uses Lewis's other books as evidence of how he embeds Christian themes in his novels: "Lewis's Space Trilogy has similar biblical allusions and theological themes to *The Lion, the Witch and the Wardrobe*."

By placing his young characters in the magical world of Narnia, Lewis is able to outline Christian theology for a young audience.

Conclusion

The final paragraph is the conclusion, restating the thesis and summarizing the arguments. The author reiterates that Aslan is a Christ figure and that Lewis uses this allusion to describe theological themes to young readers.

influenced his fiction novels. *The Lion, the Witch and the Wardrobe* is filled with biblical allusions and Aslan's construction as a Christ figure is one of the most explicit in literature. Lewis's deliberate parallel introduces complex theological themes to a children's audience.

Thinking Critically

Now it's your turn to assess the essay. Consider these questions:

1. Do you agree with the author's thesis? Is there any evidence in *The Lion, the Witch and the Wardrobe* that disproves this thesis?

2. The author states that Aslan is a Christ figure. Do you agree? Why or why not?

3. Lewis did not intend for *The Lion, the Witch and the Wardrobe* to be a biblical allegory, but many people read it as one. Does the author's intent make a difference in understanding the text?

Other Approaches

Biblical allusions in *The Lion, the Witch and the Wardrobe* can be considered in multiple ways. The previous essay is just one example of how to use biblical allusions in an analysis. Another approach might focus on Aslan's forgiveness of Edmond and how Edmond contributes to defeating the White Witch. Yet another approach could consider what the popularity of the story says about Christian values in Western culture.

Forgiveness Conquers Evil

Aslan forgives Edmond for his betrayal, releasing him from the blood oath he owes to the White Witch. After he is forgiven, Edmond seems to have more power over himself. Edmond crushes the White Witch's wand in battle, eliminating her ability to turn animals into stone. A thesis examining these ideas could be: In *The Lion, the Witch and the Wardrobe*, Aslan's forgiveness as a Christ figure allows Edmond to triumph over the White Witch, symbolically defeating evil.

Popularity Due to Christian Values

Another approach could look at the immense popularity of *The Lion, the Witch and the Wardrobe* in Western culture. The books in the series are best sellers, and the 2005 film version was immensely successful. A thesis statement for this approach could be: *The Lion, the Witch and the Wardrobe*'s popularity is a result of the prominence of the Christian worldview embedded within our society.

4

AN OVERVIEW OF
The Matrix

The Matrix is a popular 1999 science fiction movie. Praised for its cutting-edge visual effects, *The Matrix* presents a dystopian future unlike anything audiences had previously seen.

The film's main character is Thomas Anderson, a software programmer by day and a successful computer hacker known as Neo by night. At a party with one of his hacking clients, Neo meets Trinity, another famous computer hacker. Trinity tells him she knows what Neo is looking for—the answer to the question, "What is the Matrix?"[1]

The next day at work, Neo receives a package with a cell phone in it. The phone rings, and on the other end is Morpheus. He tells Neo someone is coming for him, right now in his office. Neo sees two agents, men

The Matrix was released in 1999 and became a classic science fiction film.

in suits and sunglasses. Giving him specific directions, Morpheus helps Neo escape the skyscraper office and leads him out the window to the roof. When his foot slips, Neo heads back inside and the agents arrest him.

The agents interrogate Neo, asking him about Morpheus. The head agent, Agent Smith, says he's willing to erase all of Neo's hacking criminal charges if Neo provides information about Morpheus. Neo refuses, and suddenly his mouth melts and disappears off his face. The agents hold him down and activate an electronic bug that crawls through Neo's belly button. He wakes up in his own apartment, assuming he had a nightmare.

The Red Pill and the Blue Pill

Morpheus arranges a meeting with Neo, telling him he's been looking for Neo for years. On the car ride there, Trinity uses a suction machine to extract the electronic bug from Neo. Neo panics, realizing the bug in his nightmare was real. When they meet, Morpheus tells Neo he can help him understand the Matrix. The Matrix is all around, blinding humanity from realizing they are slaves and were born into bondage. To fully understand the Matrix, Neo has a choice: he can take a blue pill or a red pill. The blue pill will make him wake up in his own

Morpheus introduces Neo to the Matrix and serves as his mentor.

bed, and the red pill will expose him to the truth of the Matrix. Neo takes the red pill.

Suddenly, a bald, pale, naked Neo wakes up in a pod of slimy water. He is attached to a web of tubes. He looks around and sees tens of thousands of pods like his. Without warning, his pod flushes into a larger body of water. As Neo passes out, Morpheus's spaceship, the *Nebuchadnezzar*, rescues him. He wakes up in a drab, dystopian reality aboard Morpheus's ship.

After recovering, Morpheus shows Neo the Matrix. Neo finds himself in a blank, malleable world, which is really a computer program accessed through the port in the back of his head. Nothing Neo knows is real. Morpheus tells Neo that the twentieth-century reality he knows is a dream. It is really several hundred years in the future. Humans developed machines with artificial intelligence and fought a war with the machines for control of the planet's energy resources. The machines won and began to grow and harvest humans as a biologic energy source. Since then, humans have been enslaved. The reality they know is the computer program known as the Matrix. Everyone is plugged into the Matrix, giving the machines the energy they need to survive. Morpheus believes Neo is the One, the person prophets say will save humanity from the Matrix and bring an end to the war with the machines. The agents Neo met are sentient programs within the Matrix that work to eliminate Morpheus and others fighting to bring down the system. They have incredible strength and are very dangerous. No one who has fought an agent has lived.

Neo learns combat by uploading computer training programs. Some of the rules of Earth, such as gravity and physics, can be bent in the Matrix. However, if someone dies in the Matrix, they also die in real life.

Cypher, another of the *Nebuchadnezzar* shipmates, sneaks into the Matrix to secretly meet with Agent

Trinity is able to leap between buildings because the rules of gravity can be bent in the Matrix.

Smith. Cypher hates the cold, gray truth of the real world. He agrees to betray Morpheus in exchange for being plugged back into the Matrix.

The Oracle's Prophecy

Morpheus takes Neo, Trinity, and others into the Matrix to meet the Oracle. The Oracle foretold that the One will bring down the Matrix, and that Morpheus would find him. As Neo meets the Oracle, she says that if he's the One, Neo will know it. The Oracle tells him that Neo's not the One, but that Morpheus will sacrifice himself to save Neo's life. Neo will have to choose between saving Morpheus or saving himself.

When they return to the phone portal out of the Matrix, Agent Smith and police officers surround the building and change the Matrix to cut off the exits.

The group tries to escape, and Morpheus attacks and distracts Agent Smith in order to give the others time to get away. Agent Smith defeats and captures Morpheus. When Neo and Trinity try to get out of the Matrix, Cypher pulls the plugs on their other shipmates and kills them. Cypher is about to kill Neo. But Tank, another crewmember, gets in the way. Tank shoots and kills Cypher. Then, Tank helps Neo and Trinity leave the Matrix.

Rescuing Morpheus

Led by Agent Smith, three agents interrogate Morpheus. They want the access codes to Zion, the last human city in the real world. Trinity and Tank are ready to pull the plug on Morpheus, killing him to save him from the agents. Neo stops them, deciding he must go back to save Morpheus. Since Morpheus thinks Neo is the One, and the Oracle told him he's not, Neo won't let Morpheus die to save him. Trinity demands to go along with Neo, noting she is now the ranking officer on the *Nebuchadnezzar.*

Trinity and Neo stage an attack on the military building where Morpheus is being held. They go to the roof to take a helicopter and fight an agent and

Morpheus is captured by Agent Smith.

other military officers. The agent shoots at Neo, but he dodges the bullets in a way that defies physics. Just as the agent is about to kill Neo, Trinity shoots the agent in the head. She's amazed at Neo's ability to dodge the agent's bullets, saying she's never seen anyone move that fast before. They take the helicopter and ambush the room where Morpheus is being held, rescuing him. Both Trinity and Morpheus escape the Matrix through a phone booth in an abandoned subway. As Neo is about to escape, Agent Smith appears and destroys the phone connection, leaving Neo no route out of the Matrix.

Instead of running, Neo stays to fight Agent Smith. He has more confidence in his own abilities, as he has discovered he's faster and stronger than other humans.

They battle in the abandoned subway, matching each other in skill. As they fight within the Matrix, sentinels, killing machines, hone in on the *Nebuchadnezzar* and attack it. The main weapon they have to defeat sentinels, an electromagnetic pulse (EMP), wipes out all electronic devices. If Tank uses it while Neo is in the Matrix, it will kill him.

The One

Neo finds another exit in an apartment building and runs to it. When he opens the apartment door to find the phone, Agent Smith is standing there. Agent Smith shoots Neo, killing him in both the Matrix and the real world. On board the ship, Trinity tells Neo's body the Oracle predicted she would fall in love with the One and that she loves Neo. In the Matrix, Neo comes back to life, bullet holes still fresh in his chest. The agents turn, shocked to find Neo alive. As they shoot at him again, Neo freezes the bullets in midair, dropping them to the ground. Back on the ship, an image of Neo suddenly appears on the ships command screens. Morpheus is amazed, announcing that Neo is the One. Agent Smith tries fighting Neo, but Neo jumps inside the agent's body and explodes Smith into hundreds of pieces.

Trinity confesses her love for Neo while he is still inside the Matrix.

The remaining agents run for their lives. Neo returns to the real world as the sentinels attack and break through the hull of the *Nebuchadnezzar*. Morpheus uses the EMP to defeat them. With all danger behind them, Trinity and Neo share a kiss.

In the final scene, Neo is speaking on a phone in the Matrix. He tells the agents this is not the end, but the beginning. He promises he will show humanity a world without rules, where anything is possible. Neo hangs up the phone and, stepping into the busy crowd of humans, flies into the sky.

5

Humanity's Savior in *The Matrix*

$\mathcal{B}$ iblical allusions in a work can be studied from many different angles. Marxist criticism is a critical approach that considers the influence of social class. An essay looking at biblical allusions in *The Matrix* through the lens of Marxist criticism would consider how biblical archetypes fit into the social structure of the work.

In *The Matrix*, Neo is extracted from the computer program known as the Matrix, discovering the life he knows is a lie. He finds his purpose is to liberate his fellow humans from the slavery to the machines, cutting off the machines' energy supply and ending the false reality of the Matrix. In *The Matrix*, Neo's construction

Neo's goal is to change the social structure of society.

Thesis Statement

The thesis statement outlines the main arguments for the essay: "In *The Matrix*, Neo's construction as Christ figure allows him to challenge and overturn societal structures within the Matrix, embodying Jesus's message of social revolution." The author will demonstrate how Neo is a Christ figure and how he upsets the status quo.

Argument One

In this argument, the author first recognizes the obvious biblical allusions in *The Matrix*: "Several character names in *The Matrix* make a direct tie to stories in the Bible."

as a Christ figure allows him to challenge and overturn societal structures within the Matrix, embodying Jesus's message of social revolution.

Several character names in *The Matrix* make a direct tie to stories in the Bible. Neo's real name, Thomas Anderson, alludes to "doubting Thomas," a disciple who does not believe Jesus has risen. Trinity refers to the Holy Trinity of God, Jesus, and the Holy Spirit. Morpheus's ship is the *Nebuchadnezzar*. In the book of Daniel, Nebuchadnezzar was a king of Babylon. However, the strongest biblical connection is Neo's construction as a Christ figure archetype.

Neo's role as the One is to liberate humanity from robot enslavement, just as Christ saves humanity from the bondage of sin. Neo fulfills his role as a Christ figure archetype—the One—through several specific character traits and plot twists. The Oracle foretold the One would come to overthrow the machines and bring down the Matrix. Similarly, the Hebrew Bible made many prophecies Christians believe Jesus Christ fulfilled. Judas betrays Jesus for 30 pieces of silver, and Cypher betrays Neo and Morpheus over a steak dinner. Most important, Neo is supposed to liberate humanity from their pod prisons, where humans are doomed to a lifetime of energy-generating slavery. He sacrifices his life for Morpheus's life, even after the Oracle tells Neo that either Morpheus will die or he will. His sacrifice, the giving of his own life to save others, is the strongest parallel to Christ in *The Matrix*. Jesus sacrifices himself on the cross to redeem humanity, offering himself up to

Argument Two

For the second argument, the author is comparing Jesus and Neo and their redemption: "Neo's role as the One is to liberate humanity from robot enslavement, just as Christ saves humanity from the bondage of sin."

Argument Three

In her third argument, the author makes another comparison between characters in the Gospels and *The Matrix*: "Morpheus acts as John the Baptist, preparing the way for Neo to challenge the Matrix."

pay the debt of sin. In their resurrections, both Neo and Jesus defeat death.

Morpheus acts as John the Baptist, preparing the way for Neo to challenge the Matrix. In the Gospels, John the Baptist is a prophet who prepares the way for Jesus Christ. He preaches about the coming of a messiah, who he later declares to be Jesus. John also baptizes Jesus in the river Jordan, where the heavens open up and a voice declares, "This is my Beloved, in whom I am well pleased."[1] According to the Oracle, Morpheus's purpose is to find the One. He spends many years searching for the One, believing Neo to be it. Morpheus helps train Neo for the rigors of fighting agents and the Matrix. They spar in their training programs, practicing many of the skills Neo will need. When Neo gets breathless during their sparring session, Morpheus challenges Neo to be stronger and faster than he is, asking Neo, "Do you think that's air you're breathing?"[2] In addition to physical training, Morpheus helps open Neo's mind

Morpheus plays a role that is similar to John the Baptist in
the Bible.

by challenging his understanding of the world around him. Morpheus parallels the role John the Baptist plays for Jesus, as one who prepares the person who will save humanity.

In this ability to change humanity, Neo reflects the social reformist teachings of Jesus. In the Bible, Jesus preaches in Galilee, a region in Israel, gaining a large following. Many of his teachings upend the social norms. In the Bible, Jesus often speaks against the established status quo upheld by religious authorities. In the Sermon on the Mount, Jesus preaches against the Old Testament rule of "an eye for an eye," instead telling people to "turn the other cheek."[3] It was considered revolutionary for Jesus to preach messages of love and forgiveness when so many religious laws at the time were about judgment and punishment. Similarly, in *The Matrix,* Neo puts the societal structure at jeopardy. In overcoming death, Neo operates outside of the rules of physics in the Matrix, changing and shaping the

Argument Four

The final argument is about challenging the rules and status quo: "In this ability to change humanity, Neo reflects the social reformist teachings of Jesus." The author relates Neo's boundary-breaking actions to Jesus's social revolutionary message.

As the One, Neo has special abilities inside the Matrix.

fabric of the world humanity lives in. At the end of the film, Neo stops a barrage of bullets midair, freezing them in place. He jumps into the body of Agent Smith, destroying him from the inside. Once he was unable to jump from building to building, but now Neo can fly. When Neo died and was resurrected as the One, he became stronger and faster and developed the ability to defy the physical limits of the Matrix. Because Neo knows the Matrix is a computer program, he does not have to follow rules such as gravity. In becoming the

Neo becomes the liberator of humanity.

One, Neo has the ability to operate outside the rules and boundaries of the Matrix and show humanity the real world. Both Neo and Jesus challenge the rules and laws of the worlds they live in, showing others how to defy the status quo.

Neo is one of the most identifiable Christ figures in modern film, specifically because of the multiple biblical allusions present in the film. His role as the liberator of humanity directly alludes to Jesus's salvation of humanity from sin. Morpheus prepares the way for Neo, the same way John the Baptist prepares for Jesus. By challenging the social structure of the Matrix, Neo reflects Jesus's revolutionary message of social equality.

Conclusion

The final paragraph concludes the essay by restating the thesis, which is supported by the evidence given in the four arguments.

Thinking Critically

Now it's your turn to assess the essay. Consider these questions:

1. Is there any evidence in *The Matrix* that disproves the author's thesis?

2. The author claims Neo is a Christ figure and Morpheus alludes to John the Baptist. Are there other characters that parallel biblical figures? How does the film make those comparisons?

3. Do Neo's physical abilities challenge the boundaries of the Matrix? Or are they unimportant since he cannot perform these feats in the real world aboard the *Nebuchadnezzar*?

Other Approaches

The previous essay is just one example of how to analyze *The Matrix*, by examining its biblical allusions. Another approach might focus on the wide array of religious influences in the film. Yet another approach might apply a feminist lens to the story, specifically by considering the strong character of Trinity.

Buddhism and Christianity in *The Matrix*

In addition to Christian themes, there are strong references to Buddhist teachings in *The Matrix*. However, as with the film's allusions to Christianity, the Buddhist components are limited. It could be argued that the film does not intend to be a direct allegory of either religious tradition. An essay that examines this issue might look at the parallel between the use of religious themes in the film and how religion affects the day-to-day life of the movie's viewers. A thesis for this approach could be: Many religions influence *The Matrix*, including Buddhism and Christianity, reflecting modern culture's tendency to loosely follow only parts of a religious tradition.

Feminist Theory in *The Matrix*

Although Trinity's name is powerful in a biblical sense, her character has less power than others in the film. Trinity is the second-in-command on the *Nebuchadnezzar*, holding an important role in the film. However, the Oracle still prophesizes she will fall in love with the One, relegating her to the role of love interest. A thesis for this approach could be: Trinity's biblical connection, being named after the Holy Trinity, does not extend to her character's role as the love interest, who lacks power and authority.

6

AN OVERVIEW OF

Lord of the Flies

*L*ord of the Flies, by William Golding, is an adventure novel with larger themes about morality and the dark side of human nature. Published in 1954, *Lord of the Flies* has become a best seller and classic for generations of young adults.

Stranded

Two boys, Ralph and Piggy, meet on the beach of an island. They have survived a plane disaster. The plane was attacked, and the pilot dropped them and other schoolboys off before it crashed. Both 12 years old, Ralph and Piggy realize quickly there are no adults on the island, just boys. As they explore, the boys discover

Lord of the Flies tells the story of a group of boys lost on an island without any adults.

a lagoon and Piggy finds a shell. Ralph uses the shell as a horn, calling the other survivors to the lagoon. Schoolchildren emerge from the jungle, including a set of twins named Sam and Eric. A whole group of boys, a choir from the plane, marches out in two lines, led by a tall boy named Jack.

The boys decide they should elect a leader. Because he blew the shell, Ralph is elected chief, although Jack is disappointed that he didn't win the vote. Ralph makes Jack the leader of the choir, and Jack declares the choir his hunters. Ralph, Jack, and Simon, another choirboy, decide to climb a nearby hill to confirm that they are on an island. The boys explore and climb the hill, flush with excitement and the thrill of being the only people on the island. As they explore the forest, Ralph, Jack, and Simon find a pig trapped in thick bushes. Jack pulls out his knife but hesitates before killing it. The pig escapes, and Jack makes excuses for not killing it when he had the chance.

Back with the group, the boys decide to use the shell as a method of keeping order—the holder of the shell has permission to speak. One of the little boys asks about a "snake-thing," and what Ralph is going to do about it.[1] The group tells him there is no beast, but

The boys learn how to hunt and cook their food.

the young boy is not convinced. Ralph tells the boys
they must start a fire to make smoke so rescue boats and
planes can see them. They climb to the top of the hill,
collecting firewood along the way. Jack grabs Piggy's
glasses and uses them to start the fire. The fire grows
large and out of control, burning miles of forest. Piggy
scolds the boys for building a rampaging fire instead of
shelters and not taking better care of the smaller boys.
Ralph, Jack, and Piggy look around, realizing they can't
find the boy who was afraid of the snake-thing.

The boys acclimate to living on the island, filling
their days with scavenging for fruit, building shelters,

swimming in the lagoon, and hunting for animals. Piggy suggests building a sundial to help them keep track of time. As they build a shelter, Ralph spots a ship on the horizon, and to his horror, finds the fire has gone out. There is no smoke for the ship to see. Jack's choirboys are supposed to keep the fire going but instead have abandoned their post. Chanting, "Kill the pig. Cut her throat. Spill her blood," the hunters proudly march back to the shelters, the carcass of a pig strung on a pole between them.[2] Ralph and Jack argue about the fire and the pig, with Ralph blaming Jack for not being rescued. Piggy yells at Jack for going hunting, and Jack hits him, sending Piggy's glasses flying off his face and breaking one lens on a rock. Jack apologizes for letting the fire go out. They eventually make up, and all warily eat the roasted pig.

The Beast

Ralph holds an assembly to try to restore order to the island, but it's run off course by the smaller boys' fear of a beast on the island. Ralph and Piggy insist there's no beast, and Jack declares he would have seen it during his hunting. The three argue about the beast and the rules.

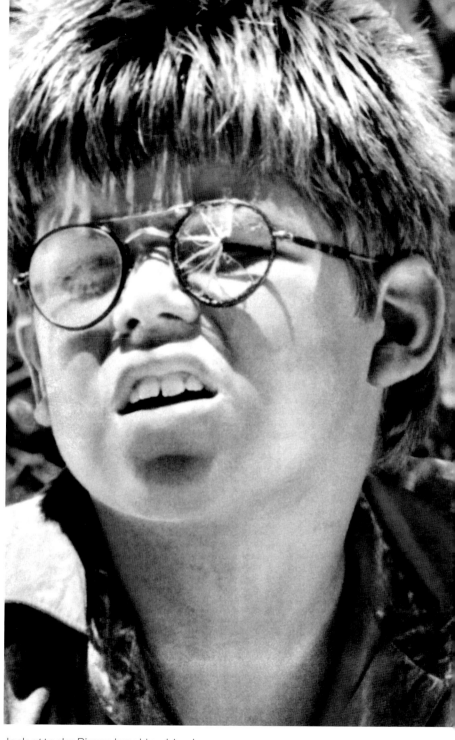

Jack attacks Piggy, breaking his glasses.

Jack yells he'll hunt the beast down, running off into the woods with his hunters.

That night, a plane explodes over the island, and a rescue parachute drifts down into the jungle and gets caught in a tree. As Sam and Eric keep early watch, they see the fabric from the parachute blowing in the wind and are frightened, thinking it's the beast. Jack, invigorated by the idea of capturing the beast, searches the island but does not find the beast. Ralph is still convinced the best thing to do is keep the fire going, but he goes along on one of Jack's hunts anyway. As he nearly kills a pig, Ralph feels the thrill of hunting, thinking maybe it's not so bad after all. They dance around pretending to hunt, with Robert, one of the choirboys, acting like the pig. In their dance, the boys actually grab and poke Robert, hurting him with their spears.

The Lord of the Flies

While on the way to restart the fire, Ralph and Jack see the body of the parachutist. They think it's the beast, and race back to tell Piggy the beast is real. The boys argue about what to do next, and Jack tries to get Ralph voted out as chief. Not enough people vote against

Ralph, so Jack angrily splits the group, taking his hunters with him. Now that the "beast" is between them and their fire on the hill, Ralph and Piggy start a fire on the beach. Meanwhile, Jack and his hunters find and kill a pig, jumping on her and violently stabbing her with their sticks. As a sacrifice to the beast, the hunters cut the head off the sow and jam it on a stick.

Simon stays behind after the hunters leave, staring at the pig's head. The pig's head becomes covered in flies, and Simon is entranced with "the Lord of the Flies."[3] He imagines the Lord of the Flies talking to him, telling him there is no beast and the Lord of the Flies is inside all of them. Simon faints. When he wakes up, he goes to examine the body of the parachutist, which is rotting while hanging from the jungle trees. He realizes it is not a beast. Simon rushes to where the boys are roasting the pig, eager to tell them the beast is not real. Jack has allowed Ralph and Piggy to eat with the hunters. As Simon approaches, the boys are playing hunter, dancing around and pretending to hunt the pig. In their ritualized hunting frenzy, the boys mistake Simon for the beast and kill him, stabbing him with sticks. Simon's body falls in the water and washes out to sea. The wind blows the parachutist out from the tree, blowing his body out to sea as well.

The next morning, Ralph, Piggy, Sam, and Eric feel guilty for getting caught up in the pig hunt and killing Simon, all pretending that they weren't really involved. In the hunter group, however, Jack thinks the beast disguised itself and that they didn't really kill it the previous night. None of the hunters acknowledge they killed Simon. Jack tells them they need to build a fire. They plan to steal the flames from Ralph's group of boys. Jack and his boys sneak up on Piggy, Ralph, Sam, and Eric and attack them, stealing Piggy's broken glasses to make a fire. Ralph's group decides to demand the glasses back from Jack, as Piggy can't see without them. The hunters capture them, and Ralph and Jack fight. Holding the shell and demanding to speak, Piggy tells them they're all acting like children and questions if they want rules and to be rescued, or just to hunt and kill. One of Jack's hunters, Roger, pushes a boulder that falls on Piggy, killing him and breaking the shell. Ralph escapes, but Sam and Eric are forced to join Jack's hunters.

Ralph hides in the jungle, trying to avoid capture by the hunters. Jack and Roger chase after him; they have a

The growing tensions meet a breaking point when Ralph and Jack fight.

stick sharpened on both ends to use on Ralph. Jack sets fire to the jungle, hoping to force Ralph out from hiding. As the hunters close in on Ralph, he desperately bursts out of hiding and runs to the beach. There on the beach is an adult, a naval officer who saw the smoke from the fire. The officer offers to rescue them. He is surprised to learn two boys were killed, thinking they should have been more civilized than that. Ralph bursts into tears, crying for Piggy and how innocent they all once were.

7

The Fall in *Lord of the Flies*

A common biblical allusion is the Fall. This is a moment discussed in the Bible when sin is born. Along with the Fall comes the idea of morality—understanding the difference between what is right and wrong or what is good and evil. Many stories make reference to the Fall. Considering how morality and the Fall are presented in a work can help us understand the moral message a work conveys.

As *Lord of the Flies* opens, the castaway schoolboys find themselves in an island paradise, one with beautiful swimming lagoons and no adults to tell them what to do. It is like the Garden of Eden in the Bible—a good

The island in *Lord of the Flies* alludes to the Garden of Eden in the Bible.

The author's thesis states: "Alluding to the Garden of Eden, *Lord of the Flies* suggests the capacity for evil is inherent within human nature." This essay discusses the nature of sin.

Argument One

In the first argument, the author draws a parallel between the island in *Lord of the Flies* and the Garden of Eden. She writes: "The island in *Lord of the Flies* is constructed as a Garden of Eden allusion."

place with a bounty of fruit and trees. As the novel progresses, it slowly changes from idyllic to terrifying as the characters become more violent, at first against wildlife and then against each other. Alluding to the Garden of Eden, *Lord of the Flies* suggests the capacity for evil is inherent within human nature.

The island in *Lord of the Flies* is constructed as a Garden of Eden allusion. In a novel, the setting can be an important component, almost as alive as a character itself. In the Bible, the Garden of Eden is a paradise God created for Adam and Eve, the first man and woman. Adam and Eve, as created by God, are perfect and without sin. In *Lord of the Flies,* the boys are stranded on a beautiful and idyllic island without adults. The boys find it to be paradise. In the first assembly, Ralph's three objectives are to have

Adam and Eve were banished from the Garden of Eden
after the Fall.

fun, make a fire, and be rescued. Ralph says, "This is our island. It's a good island. Until the grownups come to fetch us, we'll have fun."[1] Just like the Garden of Eden, the island is pristine and has all the resources they need to survive.

Unlike the single moment of the Fall, Jack and his hunters gradually lose their innocence and become more sinful the longer they are on the island as their inherent evil becomes apparent. In the Bible, God commands Adam and Eve to eat from any tree except the Tree of Knowledge. But a serpent convinces Eve to eat fruit from the Tree of Knowledge, disobeying God and bringing sin into the world. Eve gives the fruit to Adam to eat with her. As soon as they have eaten the fruit, both realize they are naked, and in their shame, they hide. This moment is known in Christian theology as the Fall, referring to Adam and Eve's fall from obedience into a state of sinfulness. After the Fall, God casts Adam and Eve out of the Garden of Eden, never allowing them to return. Thus, in the story of the Garden of Eden, there is one specific moment when Eve and Adam disobey God and leave a state of innocence.

When the Fall happens in *Lord of the Flies*, it is more gradual. Jack is a bloodthirsty, out-of-control tyrant by the end of the novel, but he didn't start that way. In Jack, Ralph, and Simon's initial survey of the island, they encounter a pig snared in a bush, unable to escape. Jack pulls his knife, ready to slice the pig. And yet he pauses, hesitant about killing the pig "because of the enormity of the knife descending and cutting into live flesh."[2] Throughout their time on the island, Ralph and Jack have disagreements about whether they should spend their time hunting or building shelters and tending the fire. At first they get angry, but they continue to make space for both activities. Ralph begrudgingly allows the hunting to continue while Jack sends some of the hunters to tend the fire.

As time goes on, Jack and the other boys lose their sense of humanity and act increasingly aggressive toward each other. Jack hits Piggy, breaking his glasses, which impairs his sight. Jack apologizes for letting the fire burn out, but not for his actions toward Piggy. The dance of pretending to catch a pig starts out friendly, but grows more and more violent. During one dance, Robert cries out and screams that the other boys are hurting him. It is the same type of dance that Simon interrupts, causing the boys to stab and claw him to death. Each action is more violent than the last, finally escalating to Piggy's intentional murder and the rabid hunt for Ralph.

The boys are not tempted to do evil things by another character, as the snake tempts Adam and Eve in the Garden of Eden. Instead, the boys make violent decisions on their own. In the Garden of Eden, a serpent tempts Adam and Eve with the forbidden fruit. The serpent, who is described as being crafty, intentionally leads the two humans into disobeying God. In *Lord of the Flies*, there is no character who tempts Jack and the other boys. As the book progresses, Jack behaves more violently and encourages the other boys to hunt and rebel against Ralph's rules. In the dance during which Simon is killed, Jack encourages

Argument Three

The author now demonstrates the lack of an outside influence in *Lord of the Flies*: "The boys are not tempted to do evil things by another character, as the snake tempts Adam and Eve in the Garden of Eden. Instead, the boys make violent decisions on their own."

The boys in *Lord of the Flies* make violent decisions on their own.

The hunters wield spears as they act out the violent tendencies already inherent in them.

Ralph and Piggy to take part, even though they aren't hunters. Piggy and Ralph participate at the edges of the circle, "eager to take a place in this demented but partly secure society."[3] As Simon approaches the group, they are described as one unit—a crowd acting against a beast that crawled out of the forest. Individually, they all decide to participate in the dance that kills Simon. Grouped together, the boys gain momentum from the frenzy of the crowd.

After Simon's death, Jack and the hunters become bolder in their violent acts. In the confrontation between the hunters and Ralph's group, Jack commands the hunters to tie up Sam and Eric, telling Ralph, "See? They do what I want."[4] But Roger decides on his own to push the rock onto Piggy as Jack and the hunters prepare to charge Ralph and Piggy with their spears. The boys' lawlessness isn't spurred on by a serpent tempting them, but instead by their own increasingly violent nature.

Simon's discovery that the Lord of the Flies is not real, but instead a manifestation of their own imaginations, proves that Jack and the hunters' savage behavior already existed in their natures. Seeing the sow's head covered in flies, Simon has a transcendental moment while staring into its eyes. The Lord of the Flies talks to him, mocking him for being different from the other boys. He taunts Simon, saying, "Fancy thinking the Beast was something you could hunt and kill! . . . You knew, didn't you? I'm part of you?"[5] In making his way to the camp on the beach, Simon comes across the parachutist's body, rotting while hanging from the jungle trees. He recognizes it for what it is and is not afraid of the beast. To him, the beast can't cause any harm. Simon knows

Argument Four

The final argument shows the beast is not real, and the boys' human natures led them to violence: "Simon's discovery that the Lord of the Flies is not real, but instead a manifestation of their own imaginations, proves that Jack and the hunters' savage behavior already existed in their natures."

he must tell the others about his discovery. If there's no real beast, then the motivation for Jack's behavior is completely unfounded. There's no need to hunt and kill the beast, because it's not real. Instead, the desire for destruction and violence originated within the boys.

Lord of the Flies presents two alternative images—an island paradise and a dystopian nightmare. The story starts in a paradise. But the gradual loss of innocence and increase in aggressive behavior turns it into a nightmare. Unlike the Garden of Eden, this change comes not from a sudden incident, but a steady loss of morality. This confirms that the potential for evil always existed within each of the boys, even before they arrived on the island. The beast is not outside, but inside and part of humanity.

Conclusion

The last paragraph ends the critique, bringing back the image of an island paradise compared with a nightmare. The author restates the thesis and previous arguments.

Thinking Critically

Now it's your turn to assess the essay. Consider these questions:

1. Do you agree with the author's thesis? Is there any evidence that disproves this theory?

2. What parts of the essay were most convincing? What parts were least convincing?

3. The author focuses mainly on Ralph, Jack, and Simon as indicators of the increase in aggressive behavior, but Piggy is also a central character in the novel. Is there any evidence in Piggy's actions that proves or disproves this argument?

Other Approaches

A critique can be applied to a book in many different ways. The previous essay is just one example of how to use biblical allusions in a critique. Another way of approaching *Lord of the Flies* is through the lens of Simon, who has been called a Christ figure. Yet another approach might consider the political systems various characters represent.

Simon as Incomplete Christ Figure

Simon has been called a Christ figure in other analyses of *Lord of the Flies*, which mention his role as an outcast and realization of the true nature of the beast. However, Simon does not provide redemption for the boys. A thesis statement for this argument could be: Simon's confrontation with the Lord of the Flies is similar to Jesus's temptation during his 40 days in the desert; however, his death does not lead to salvation for the rest of the boys as it would if he was a true Christ figure.

Symbolism in Political Systems

Recognizing biblical allusions in *Lord of the Flies* can call other social structures into question. For example, you might consider the text as a lesson in how people are successfully governed. In the book, Ralph and Jack symbolize different political systems, democracy and totalitarianism respectively. A thesis statement for this argument could be: In layering symbolism and biblical allusions, Golding implies that dictatorships expose the sinful side of human nature.

8

AN OVERVIEW OF
The Lion King

The Lion King is a popular Disney movie, released in 1994, that tells the story of Simba, a lion who must figure out his identity and his role in the animal hierarchy. The movie's plot is drawn from several sources, including Shakespeare's play *Hamlet* and the Bible. Like *Hamlet*, *The Lion King* includes an uncle who kills the main character's father. Biblical influences include the story of Moses, the king of Egypt who goes into exile and returns to free his people, and the story of Joseph, who is sold into slavery by his brothers and becomes a powerful man in Egypt, who in turn helps his brothers during a famine.

The Lion King focuses on the story of Simba, a young lion in line to become king.

The Circle of Life

As the sun rises on the savanna, animals from across the land come to Pride Rock to see the newborn lion cub. Rafiki, the baboon shaman, meets Mufasa and Sarabi, the proud parents of the new cub, and prepares the cub for his presentation. Rafiki walks to the end of Pride Rock and presents the new cub, Simba, to the crowd of animals. Later on, Mufasa visits his brother, Scar, to find out why he missed Simba's presentation ceremony. Accompanied by Zazu, his assistant, Mufasa tells Scar that Simba will one day be his king, and he must respect him. Moody and rude, Scar warns Mufasa to watch his back and then sulks off.

As Simba grows, he becomes an energetic and curious cub. One day, Mufasa takes Simba to the top of Pride Rock to watch the sunrise. There, they talk about how Simba will one day rule the Pride Lands. Mufasa explains how everything exists together. A king must respect all the animals and how they live together in the circle of life. After Mufasa rushes off to protect the Pride Lands from hyenas, Simba goes to see Scar. He brags about how he'll be king one day. Scar, being deceitful, makes Simba promise to never go to the

As a young club, Simba gets into trouble often.

elephant graveyard, saying only brave lions go there.
Intrigued by Scar's words, Simba recruits his best friend,
Nala, to go to the graveyard with him. Simba's mother
sends Zazu along to babysit.

The Elephant Graveyard

Zazu's gleeful that Simba and Nala get along so well, as
they are betrothed to be married one day. Simba
promises to get rid of that rule as soon as he's king.
Simba and Nala manage to lose Zazu and go to the
elephant graveyard by themselves. As they play and
wrestle, Nala pins Simba twice in a row, and they
tumble into the elephant graveyard. Full of giant bones,
the elephant graveyard is eerie. Zazu catches up to
them, telling them they're all in danger in the elephant

graveyard. Simba doesn't take his warning seriously, laughing at Zazu.

Shenzi, Banzai, and Ed, three hyenas, jump out from behind a skull and corner Simba, Nala, and Zazu. They chase them around the elephant graveyard, trying to catch the lions. Eventually, the hyenas trap the lion cubs in a corner. Mufasa comes to their rescue, scaring the hyenas away. Mufasa is disappointed in Simba, telling him truly brave lions don't need to go looking for trouble to prove they're brave. Together, they look up at the star-filled sky. Mufasa tells Simba if he's ever lonely, he should look up at the stars and know they're lights from the great lion kings of the past.

Scar goes to the elephant graveyard to meet with Shenzi, Banzai, and Ed. Scar wants to know why the hyenas didn't kill Simba and Nala, telling them they should have killed Mufasa too. Scar comes up with a plan to kill Mufasa and Simba, allowing him to take the throne.

The next day, Scar lures Simba to the gorge, telling him Mufasa has a surprise for him. The hyenas start a stampede of wildebeests, which run down into the gorge and put Simba's life in danger. Scar tells Mufasa Simba's in the gorge. Mufasa rushes to rescue him. Mufasa finds

Simba and carries him to safety. As Mufasa himself tries to climb out of the gorge, Scar meets him and pushes him back into the stampede. Simba finds Mufasa's body, and Scar convinces him it's Simba's fault Mufasa died. Scar tells him to run away, and the hyenas chase Simba out of the Pride Lands to kill him. Simba escapes, running through a patch of thorns. With Mufasa dead, Scar and the hyenas take over the Pride Lands.

Hakuna Matata

Simba passes out in the desert and is rescued by Timon, a meerkat, and Pumbaa, a warthog. They tell Simba to put his past behind him and teach him *hakuna matata*, which means "no worries." They take him to the jungle, where they live together and eat bugs. Simba grows up with Timon and Pumbaa, becoming an adult lion.

At Pride Rock, Scar has driven the kingdom into the ground. The savanna has been overhunted, throwing the circle of life out of balance. The lionesses cannot find anything to hunt. Scar is sensitive, not allowing anyone to say Mufasa's name in his presence.

Simba enjoys life with Timon and Pumbaa, eating bugs and not worrying about anything. One day, a lioness attacks Pumbaa. Simba fights her, saving

Simba becomes friends with Timon and Pumbaa.

Pumbaa's life. Simba recognizes Nala when she pins him
to the ground, just like when they were kids. Nala tells
him about Scar ruling the Pride Lands, explaining all of
the lionesses think Simba's dead. Simba is reluctant to
go back to the Pride Lands, thinking everyone blames
him for Mufasa's death. He doesn't want to be king. Nala
and Simba spend time together, playing in the jungle
and falling in love. Nala doesn't understand why Simba
doesn't want to go back to Pride Rock, telling him Scar
is ruining the Pride Lands and they'll soon run out of
food. She tells Simba it's his responsibility to be king and
reclaim the Pride Lands from the hyenas. They argue,
with Simba refusing to go back. He storms off, blaming

himself for what happened to Mufasa. Rafiki, the baboon shaman, finds Simba and takes him to find the ghost of Mufasa. The ghost tells Simba he has forgotten his past, and he must go back and be the one true king. Simba decides he must go back and face Scar. Nala, Timon, and Pumbaa decide to follow him and help him fight for Pride Rock.

Return to Pride Rock

When Simba returns, he finds the Pride Lands decimated. The land is overhunted and in a drought, with animal skeletons littered across the land. As Simba sneaks up, Scar is holding a meeting, asking Sarabi why the lionesses are not hunting. She tells him there is no food and they should leave Pride Rock. When Sarabi insults Scar, calling him half the lion Mufasa was, he strikes her, knocking her to the ground. Simba jumps to Sarabi's aid, and both Sarabi and Scar are surprised to see Simba alive. Lightning strikes the dried grass and bushes near Pride Rock, starting a raging fire. Simba demands Scar step down as king, but Scar insists the hyenas won't let him. Scar tells the lionesses that Simba murdered Mufasa, forcing him to admit he's responsible for Mufasa's death. Scar backs Simba off the ledge at

Pride Rock and whispers in Simba's ear that he killed Mufasa. Enraged, Simba jumps up, pinning Scar and making him admit he killed Mufasa. The lionesses join the fight, outraged at Scar's confession. The hyenas step up to fight for Scar. Simba follows Scar up to the top of Pride Rock, where Scar begs for mercy. He blames the hyenas, saying it was entirely their idea. Simba tells him to run away and never return, echoing the words Scar told Simba as a young cub. Scar swipes hot coals into Simba's eyes, and they fight a ferocious battle. Simba knocks Scar off the edge, where the hyenas corner Scar and attack him.

As the battle ends, rain falls and puts out the blazing fire. Simba is reunited with Sarabi, Nala, and the other lionesses. Simba climbs to the edge of Pride Rock, taking his rightful role as king. With Simba as king, the Pride Lands return to their healthy and green state, and the herds return. The circle of life is restored, and later, Simba, Nala, Rafiki, Timon, and Pumbaa present Simba and Nala's newborn cub to the animal herds.

Simba returns to Pride Rock to take the throne from Scar.

Lionesses and the New Testament

$\mathcal{B}$iblical allusions in text can bring to the forefront interesting questions about gender roles and the patriarchal structures of society. Gender roles are traditional ideas about how men and women should behave as a result of their genders. Throughout much of history, men's roles and experiences have been prioritized and highlighted. Considering how women were discussed in the Bible and in the works of today can help us understand the downfalls of a patriarchal society.

A smashing success, *The Lion King* shaped childhood experiences and future Disney movies for a generation. It used many sources as plot inspiration, including

The plot of *The Lion King* focuses on male experiences.

the biblical story of Moses. In this story, the women around Moses act courageously to help and protect him. Unfortunately, *The Lion King's* male-centered plot contributes to maintaining the patriarchal structures of society. Although the biblical story of Moses has female characters with agency, the narrative of *The Lion King* keeps the female lions in a submissive role to maintain patriarchal dominance.

The Lion King alludes to the biblical story of Moses, who led the Israelites out of bondage in Egypt and to the Promised Land. Moses, like Simba, is a prince. When he witnesses an Egyptian beating a Hebrew laborer, Moses becomes angry and kills the Egyptian. He goes into exile in the desert, leaving behind his life as a prince in Egypt. After several years, God speaks to Moses through the burning bush,

Thesis Statement

The author states her thesis: "Although the biblical story of Moses has female characters with agency, the narrative of *The Lion King* keeps the female lions in a submissive role to maintain patriarchal dominance."

Argument One

First, the author draws the parallels between the story of Moses and *The Lion King*. The argument is: "*The Lion King* alludes to the biblical story of Moses, who led the Israelites out of bondage in Egypt and to the Promised Land."

calling him to return to Egypt and liberate his fellow Israelites from slavery. Moses returns and God casts ten plagues on Egypt, wearing down the pharaoh until he agrees to free the Israelites. Moses leads them across the Red Sea and toward the Promised Land. *The Lion King* alludes to this story as the exiled prince returns to liberate his people.

Even from a young age, Simba is weaker and less responsible than Nala. *The Lion King* focuses on Simba as the main character because of the tendency of monarchies to pass ruling authority from father to son. However, Simba is portrayed as a young, naïve lion cub with a lot to learn about responsibility before he takes over as king. Even though Mufasa specifically tells Simba not to go to the elephant graveyard, his curiosity is too strong. Egged on by Scar, Simba is tricked into thinking he should go to the elephant graveyard because that's what brave lions do. As a result, Simba puts both himself and Nala in danger. As an adult, Simba avoids

Argument Two

The author argues that female characters in *The Lion King* do not have agency even though their abilities are sometimes superior to those of the male characters. The argument is: "Even from a young age, Simba is weaker and less responsible than Nala."

Nala, *left*, is more responsible than Simba, even when they are both young.

returning to Pride Rock because he's ashamed, thinking he caused Mufasa's death. After Nala discovers him in the jungle and tells him about the struggles she, Sarabi, and the other lionesses are having at Pride Rock, Simba refuses to go back. Nala even cites his responsibility as the next king, telling Simba his behavior is nothing like his father's. Eventually, Simba decides to return to Pride Rock and face his uncle. However, for most of the movie Simba is irresponsible, and his actions put both himself and others in harm's way.

Nala, on the other hand, is much more responsible than Simba. As an adult lioness, Nala helps provide food and protection for the other lions in the pride. That is her role in the hierarchy within the lion pride. As Scar has destroyed and overhunted the Pride Lands, the lionesses have to travel farther and farther to find food. When she discovers Simba in the jungle, Nala is out hunting for food to bring back to keep the lionesses from starving. Nala reminds Simba of his responsibility to his mother, to the lion pride, and to the Pride Lands. She holds him accountable for his years of exile, telling Simba he must take his rightful role as king of the Pride Lands.

Nala is also stronger than Simba. When they tumble and wrestle as young lion cubs, Nala pins Simba twice, once in the savanna and once in the elephant graveyard. She is portrayed as stronger and a better fighter than Simba. As adults, they fight again the first time they meet. The movie portrays this fight as intense. Nala is trying to hunt food for her starving pride, while Simba is fighting to protect Pumbaa's life. Even in this high stakes situation, Nala pins Simba by the shoulders, clearly winning the fight. Although Simba is shown to be a fierce fighter, Nala is repeatedly proven stronger, faster, and better in fights.

Argument Three

The author shows how *The Lion King* focuses on male experiences. The third argument is: "Although they are strong and able, the lionesses do not overthrow Scar."

Although they are strong and able, the lionesses do not overthrow Scar. The pride is large, consisting of many lionesses. Nala, as demonstrated, is both strong and an excellent fighter. They know they are starving and must leave the Pride Lands to survive. And yet, they do not step out of their gendered roles as food providers to overthrow Scar. A plotline featuring Nala as the Pride Lands' rescuer instead of Simba would overturn the story's implicit patriarchal structure.

By focusing the movie on Simba, *The Lion King* demonstrates the patriarchal notion that male experiences are more universal than female ones, and ultimately more important.

Argument Four

The author turns back to the story of Moses. She argues that in this story, the female characters take action.
The fourth argument is: "In comparison to the lionesses, Moses's mother and his sister, Miriam, protect Moses from the pharaoh's decree to kill all Jewish sons, highlighting their roles as strong female characters."

In comparison to the lionesses, Moses's mother and his sister, Miriam, protect Moses from the

When the pharaoh's daughter finds Moses, Miriam comes up with a plan to bring Moses back to his mother.

pharaoh's decree to kill all Jewish sons, highlighting their roles as strong female characters. In Exodus, the pharaoh is fearful of the growing population of Israelites in Egypt. He rules that all newborn Israelite boys be thrown in the Nile River, controlling the growing Israelite population while instilling fear and terror in the Israelite community. Moses's mother does not want her newborn son to die, so she hides him. With Miriam, Moses's mother places him in a basket and sends him floating down the Nile, hidden by reeds. The pharaoh's daughter sees the basket in the reeds and claims the baby as her own. Miriam watches this occur, and she asks the pharaoh's daughter if she should find a nurse to feed and take care of the baby. The pharaoh's daughter says yes, and Miriam brings Moses back to his mother, who takes care of him until he is old enough to live in the palace. Both Moses's mother and Miriam take courageous action to protect the life of their son and brother. They disobey the pharaoh's decree, and their actions put the whole family in jeopardy. However, their bold actions save Moses's life. Additionally, Miriam's offer to the pharaoh's daughter to find a nurse for the baby allows Moses to grow up with his own family. These two strong female characters protect Moses from certain death.

Even though *The Lion King* is based on the story of Moses, which contains several strong female characters such as Moses's mother and Miriam, it upholds a patriarchal system. Nala is repeatedly shown as more responsible, stronger, and a better fighter than Simba, yet she does not overthrow Scar. She is unhappy with Scar's rule, but does not challenge the system that allows him to rule in the first place. By centering *The Lion King* on Simba, he becomes the primary character through which the audience experiences the story.

Conclusion

The conclusion restates the thesis and summarizes the arguments made in support of the thesis.

Thinking Critically

Now it's your turn to assess the essay. Consider these questions:

1. Do you think *The Lion King* has a patriarchal point of view? What evidence is there for and against this idea?

2. What parts of the essay were most convincing? What parts were least convincing?

3. How do *The Lion King*'s biblical allusions contribute to the author's thesis?

Other Approaches

A critique can be applied to a book in many different ways. The previous essay is just one example of how to use biblical allusions in a critique. Another approach might compare Simba's exile into the desert to Moses's exile. A second approach could look at the movie's ecological message and what it says about being stewards of the earth.

Exile into the Desert

Another part of Moses's story is his departure from Egypt to spend many years in the desert. He returns to challenge the pharaoh to release the Israelites from slavery. A thesis for this approach could be: Simba's exile from Pride Rock mirrors Moses's exile into the desert, where both characters have revelatory experiences that shape their leadership in reclaiming their rightful authority.

Ecotheology and *The Lion King*

Scar allows the hyenas to hunt the herds in the Pride Lands, throwing off the balance in the circle of life. Many times in the Bible, humans are instructed to be good stewards of Earth's natural resources. A thesis statement for a critique that uses this approach could be: The ecological destruction of the Pride Lands teaches children about exploiting natural resources and instills the biblical value of being good stewards of Earth.

Analyze It!

Now that you have examined the theme of biblical allusions, are you ready to perform your own analysis? You have read that this type of evaluation can help you look at literature in a new way and make you pay attention to certain issues you may not have otherwise recognized. So, why not look for biblical allusions in one or more of your favorite books?

First, choose the work you want to analyze. What biblical allusions are present in the work? Do the characters remind you of people that appear in the Bible? How do the allusions affect your opinion of the story? If you choose to compare the biblical allusions in more than one work, what do they have in common? How do they differ? Next, write a specific question about the theme that interests you. Then you can form your thesis, which should provide the answer to that question. Your thesis is the most important part of your analysis and offers an argument about the work, considering the theme, its effect on the characters, or what it says about society or the world. Recall that the thesis statement typically appears at the very end of the introductory paragraph of your essay. It is usually only one sentence long.

After you have written your thesis, find evidence to back it up. Good places to start are in the work itself or in journals or articles that discuss what other people have said about it. You may also want to read about the author or creator's life so you can get a sense of what factors may have affected the creative process. This can be especially useful if you are considering how the theme connects to history or the author's intent.

You should also explore parts of the book that seem to disprove your thesis and create an argument against them. As you do this, you might want to address what others have written about the book. Their quotes may help support your claim.

Before you start analyzing a work, think about the different arguments made in this book. Reflect on how evidence supporting the thesis was presented. Did you find that some of the techniques used to back up the arguments were more convincing than others? Try these methods as you prove your thesis in your own critique.

When you are finished writing your critique, read it over carefully. Is your thesis statement understandable? Do the supporting arguments flow logically, with the topic of each paragraph clearly stated? Can you add any information that would present your readers with a stronger argument in favor of your thesis? Were you able to use quotes from the book, as well as from other critics, to enhance your ideas? Did you see the work in a new light?

Glossary

agency
The state of having power or authority.

agnosticism
The belief that religious claims are unknown and unable to be proven true.

allegory
A story that teaches the reader a moral or religious lesson.

apologetics
A theology that defends Christianity using reason.

atheism
The rejection of belief in the existence of gods and goddesses.

atonement
A theological concept that describes how humans are reconciled with God.

dystopia
A place where everything is bad and people have terrible lives.

idyllic
Peaceful and beautiful.

inherent
Existing within something.

manifestation
Something that originates in one's mind and becomes real.

patriarchy
A society in which men dominate.

pristine
Untouched.

sentient
Able to feel things.

shaman
A healer who uses magic.

status quo
Current state.

transcendental
Supernatural.

Characteristics
AND CLASSICS

Biblical allusions are a common theme in literature. Because there are many stories in the Bible, there are many parallels that can occur.

This theme often includes:

- Parallels to people in the Bible, such as Christ, Moses, Noah, and others
- Parallels to specific Bible stories, such as the Fall in Genesis
- Parallels to biblical locations, such as the Garden of Eden and Babylon
- Concepts of sin, evil, and Satan

Some famous works with biblical allusions are:

- Frances Hodgson Burnett's *The Secret Garden*
- Disney's *Snow White*
- J. R. R. Tolkien's Lord of the Rings trilogy
- Douglas Adams's *The Hitchhiker's Guide to the Galaxy*
- J. K. Rowling's Harry Potter series
- Cormac McCarthy's *The Road*

References

Golding, William. *Lord of the Flies*. New York: Penguin, 1954. Print.

Higgins, James E. "A Letter From C. S. Lewis." *The Horn Book Magazine*. Oct. 1966. Web. 24 Nov. 2014.

Jacobs, Alan. *The Narnian: The Life and Imagination of C. S. Lewis*. New York: Harper, 2005. Print.

Lang, J. Stephen. *Everyday Biblical Literacy: The Essential Guide to Biblical Allusions in Art, Literature and Life*. Cincinnati, OH: Writer's Digest, 2007. Print.

Lewis, C. S. *The Collected Letters of C. S. Lewis II*. San Francisco, CA: Harper, 2005. Print.

Lewis, C. S. *The Lion, the Witch and the Wardrobe*. New York: Harper, 1950. Print.

The Lion King. Dir. Roger Allers, Rob Minkoff. Walt Disney Pictures, 1994. DVD.

The Matrix. Dir. The Wachowskis. Warner Brothers Films, 1999. DVD.

The New Oxford Annotated Bible, Third Edition. Ed. Michael Coogan. New York: Oxford UP, 2001. Print.

Reinhartz, Adele. *Jesus of Hollywood*. New York: Oxford UP, 2007. Print.

Saunders, Ben. *Do The Gods Wear Capes?: Spirituality, Fantasy and Superheroes*. London: Bloomsbury Academic, 2011. Print.

Additional
RESOURCES

Further Readings

Brennan, Herbid, ed. *Through the Wardrobe: Your Favorite Authors on C. S. Lewis's Chronicles of Narnia.* Dallas, TX: BenBella, 2010. Print.

Bryfonski, Dedria. *Violence in William Golding's* Lord of the Flies. Detroit, MI: Greenhaven, 2010. Print

Yeffeth, Glenn, ed. *Taking the Red Pill: Science, Philosophy, and Religion in the Matrix.* Dallas, TX: BenBella, 2003. Print.

Websites

To learn more about Essential Literary Themes, visit **booklinks.abdopublishing.com**. These links are routinely monitored and updated to provide the most current information available.

Places to Visit

C. S. Lewis Study Center at the Kilns
C. S. Lewis Foundation
1725 Orange Tree Lane, Suite C
Redlands, CA 92374
909-793-0949
http://www.cslewis.org
This Christian organization seeks to teach and inspire other
Christians students, teachers, artists, and scholars.

International Conference on Religion & Film
University of Nebraska – Omaha
http://www.unomaha.edu/2014religionfilm
Scholars present their research about religion in film at this annual
international conference.

The Walt Disney Family Museum
104 Montgomery Street
San Francisco, CA 94129
415-345-6800
http://www.waltdisney.org
This museum provides information about Walt Disney, the founder
of Walt Disney Pictures, which produced *The Lion King* and many
other popular animated films.

Source Notes

Chapter 1. Introduction to Themes in Literature

None.

Chapter 2. An Overview of *The Lion, the Witch and the Wardrobe*

1. C. S. Lewis. *The Lion, the Witch and the Wardrobe*. New York: Harper, 2003. Print. 169.

Chapter 3. C. S. Lewis and Author Intent

1. C. S. Lewis. *The Lion, the Witch and the Wardrobe*. New York: Harper, 2005.
Print. 86.
2. Matthew 26:42
3. James E. Higgins. "A Letter From C. S. Lewis." *Horn Book Magazine*. Oct. 1966. Web. 24 Nov. 2014.
4. C. S. Lewis. *The Collected Letters of C. S. Lewis II*. San Francisco: Harper, 2005. Print. 262.

Chapter 4. An Overview of *The Matrix*

1. *The Matrix*. Dir. The Wachowskis. Warner Brothers Films, 1999. DVD.

Chapter 5. Humanity's Savior in *The Matrix*

1. Matthew 3:13–17.
2. *The Matrix*. Dir. The Wachowskis. Warner Brothers Films, 1999. DVD.
3. Matthew 5:38–39.

Chapter 6. An Overview of *Lord of the Flies*

1. William Golding. *Lord of the Flies*. New York: Penguin, 1954. Print. 35.
2. Ibid. 69.
3. Ibid. 138.

Chapter 7. The Fall in *Lord of the Flies*

1. William Golding. *Lord of the Flies*. New York: Penguin, 1954. Print. 35.
2. Ibid. 31.
3. Ibid. 152.
4. Ibid. 179.
5. Ibid. 207.

Chapter 8. An Overview of *The Lion King*

None.

Chapter 9. Lionesses and the New Testament

None.

Index

About the Author

Lindsay Bacher has a bachelor of arts degree in English and religion from Hamline University and a master of art and religion degree from Yale Divinity School. She has presented research on Christ figures in film at a national academic conference. She lives in Minneapolis, Minnesota, with her husband and two dogs, Sam and Maggie.